I0791478

# The WOMAN in ME

## OMOYIE FAITH KALU

BALBOA.PRESS

A DIVISION OF HAY HOUSE

Balboa Press books may be ordered through booksellers or by contacting:

Balboa Press
A Division of Hay House
1663 Liberty Drive
Bloomington, IN 47403
www.balboapress.co.uk
UK TFN: 0800 0148647 (Toll Free inside the UK)
UK Local: (02) 0369 56325 (+44 20 3695 6325 from outside the UK)



Print information available on the last page.

ISBN: 978-1-9822-8634-7 (sc)
ISBN: 978-1-9822-8633-0 (e)

Balboa Press rev. date: 08/30/2022

To every woman out there who needs to be exceptional
and successful. It's all about you, sweetheart.

# Contents

# Acknowledgements

I would like to thank my family, friends, and everyone who contributed actively and passively to the success of this project *Woman in Me*. Special thanks to my darling husband, who put up with me throughout the arduous process of writing this book. For your sacrifice and patience, I am grateful. Finally, special thanks to Almighty God for everything.

# 1

# Woman: The Perfectionist

A perfectionist is someone who is persistent in refusing to accept any standard short of perfection. This is a good definition of "woman". The word "perfection" is rationale, but with regard to women, perfection is not perfect.

A woman is created with special abilities that can be likened to gold or diamonds. Gold and diamonds are precious materials that are loved by all. They are very expensive and never lose value. They are always precious to behold, and there is something unique about them. They are hidden treasures and always protected. They are obtained through the most difficult system of excavation and purification. They are hidden deep in the earth and go through a difficult process of transformation to achieve their ultimate beauty. They are perfect materials, but are they really perfect? No!

The above illustration is likened to a woman. We carefully consider the unique abilities that make up a woman in subsequent chapters. Most times, we are too busy with career, work, and other life activities that we never get to take a break to reflect or ponder the questions that can put us in the right direction for life. This is why we struggle too much and, thereby, deny ourselves the sweetness of earth. We never give ourselves the chance to know who we really are and what the earth has to offer us. This may contribute to the rising deterioration of health in women.

We never stop to ask ourselves what makes us, *us*? Why am I called "woman"? What are my natural abilities? What's my duty to earth? Not just to one's family. What can I do to be that imperfect perfectionist?

Perfection is a consistent effort to do what is right. It's like a doctor practising medicine. The doctor may make mistakes sometimes, but he or she should grow through it and keep practising. A lawyer sometimes loses cases, but he or she learns from it and continues practising. You must keep practising being perfect.

# 2

## The African Experience

Learn from the African experience. Pick up your bag of right thinking and move on.

Growing up as a female in Africa is like a movie being underrated despite a huge budget. Most times it is a sour experience you may never get to understand, yet it used to be the only mechanism. It may have gotten better now, which means more liberty for a child growing up under an African parent. But do you know that training a female child in school is considered worthless? It was generally believed that even if girls received the highest level of education, they would still end up in a man's kitchen, cooking and serving the family. You don't have the right to tell your husband what should be done in the house. You don't even get to talk when he is talking. When he is angry and approaches you about it, even if he is the offender, you will bow your head to the floor and not respond or say anything except if asked a question or permitted to talk.

When you wake up in the morning, you get on your knees to greet him. If you must talk to him, you address him with exalted pet names like, "my lord", and "daddy". "My lord, what would you prefer for breakfast?" When he is angry and shouting, you don't get to talk back. If you do, his kinsmen will invite you to meet with them, and they will tell you what to bring them as a penalty for your action. You may be required to bring a he-goat or pay a specific sum that's equivalent to a he-goat. This makes the growing female child look somewhat worthless compared to a male child. As such, no parent wants to end up training a female child who will definitely end up as a servant to a man. Though this practice may have been reduced drastically in African society, it's still widely practised.

This system was believed to be the only way society would respect a female child or woman and the only way a woman could be virtuous. What were the intentions of the parents? Do you think they hated their female children? If you think the answer is yes, you should know what happens to a man if he is found close to a female child who is still under her parents' care, regardless of her age. I think it's rather because they love the female child too much. As such, her parents want to protect her and make her a responsible child, but the approach speaks the opposite. The approach is intended to bring out the woman in you, but it's a crude system. What is important are the intentions: bringing out the woman in you.

In today's society, the approach has changed. On the face of it, things seem to get better with these same intentions. But the result most times is appalling. What went wrong? Do you think parents don't try to curtail the natural excesses of their female children? Do you think the internet and advancements in technology are overwhelming our abilities to model our female children to be responsible enough? Considering these questions, one will be tempted to say yes. Most parents have lost it due to the rising cost of living, their careers, too many responsibilities, and the list goes on. Most parents care less about their female children. The parents don't teach them from their experiences as children and then adults. Instead, parents allow their children to learn from their experiences. Parents forget those experiences will always leave marks or traumatize their children. If you teach them from *your* experiences, they will never leave a mark. So which is better?

If you grew up like this, it's time to stop and think. You may have lost the woman in you. Or perhaps you don't know how to bring out that perfection, that special gift of a woman, that special ability. Follow me now, and become that woman who knows how to charge her existence, impact her generation, and print a legacy on time.

# 3

## Direction

In a world that is controlled by different philosophical views, what you give your attention to the most will usually give you direction. You should ask yourself some important questions on a regular basis:

> What gives you direction?
>
> Do you pay too much attention to make-up and how you look?
>
> Do you spend your free time watching movies on the internet?
>
> When on the internet, what content do you spend most of your time on?
>
> Are you building yourself, or are you busy commenting and sharing celebrity content?
>
> What effort are you putting into getting value and improving yourself?
>
> What types of friends do you have?
>
> What does your circle of friends discuss often?

> Have you ever thought about what you can do
> to repair a situation you keep complaining
> about?
> Are you proud of the things you do?
> Are you proud of the girl or woman you have
> become? If not, what efforts to improve do
> you have on the table?

These questions and more should guide your choices in life and redirect you when you are derailing because truly, as a woman, you have more responsibilities, and that requires more attention. Society needs your impact, your environment needs your contributions, and the younger generation needs your moral values to lean on. You can't just sit back and waste away. You have to pick up your bag and start that journey.

Do you know that as a woman, you were designed to solve problems? You were designed to cover the holes where men fail. You were designed to absorb uncertainties and make headway with them. You were designed to stand in the gap between humanity and nature. You were designed to be perfect in weakness, perfect in strength, perfect in anything good for you, your family, and your immediate environment. All you need to do is look deep inside and remind yourself that you are an imperfect perfectionist. So when you make mistakes, do not worry. When you fail, do not worry. When you find yourself fighting that addiction, do not worry. After all, you are imperfect perfectionist. You keep pushing for the best. You don't stay put and lament or cry all day and all night because you know that doesn't change a thing. Pick up your bag and pursue perfection.

Yes, you can achieve it if you can think it. Don't be limited by what you think or what your society says about women. It is what *you* say that matters. This is your world, so live it. It is your time, so spend it. It is your duty, so serve it. It is your decision, so make it. The world needs you to shape it. If you don't, who will?

In my definition, "woman" means strength, courage, respect, perfection, enthusiasm, compassion, intelligence, beauty, and above all, humanity. Now you know this is you, so start digging out from you what makes you a woman. Don't expect anybody to do this for you. Start to live right. Put behind you every anti-woman attitude. Yes, you can.

# 4

# Woman: Your Natural Abilities

As a woman, you possess several abilities you may not know about. They are hidden deep inside you. You require special attention and effort to learn how to use these inborn abilities every woman possesses. Yes, you have them inside you. Stop allowing bad character traits to surface. Barricade them. Do not allow dirty manners. Avoid selfish interests. Do not allow people who have even bigger problems feed you with malnourished advice. Run from people who tell you bad stuff about other people or make you feel you and your family aren't trying hard enough. Read good books that tell you the truth and how to excavate the deep things inside you. I encourage you to read my other book, *Who Am I?*

*Perfect Multitasking*

Multitasking is the performance of multiple tasks at one time. Many women do not know nature gave them this ability. Taking advantage of this ability can improve your domestic productivity, thereby adding value to your life.

A resource from mheducation said, "In many ways, multitasking seems like a good idea: by working on more than one task at once, multitaskers are theoretically more productive. You can be cooking, watching the kids, and doing Laundry at the same time."

This is a unique ability not everyone realizes she has. If you have never tried to be a superwoman in your home, you are wasting a special gift. Try it now; you will be happy you did. But don't go overboard. If you do, men may see it as something regular or normal and take advantage of it.

## Deep as the Ocean

My grandmother was a very hardworking woman. She would wake up as early as 4:30 a.m. every day; she never missed it. After preparing the meal and getting all the grandchildren ready for school, she would leave instructions on what we must do, where to pick some money, and what to do when we returned from school. Then she left for our farm, about five miles away, but not without our grandfather, whose duty was to use the horsewhip to correct us when we went wrong.

Almost every day, my grandfather always annoyed his wife. When they came back, they argued over issues no one ever understood, trivial issues. My grandfather was a bit temperamental. As the quarrel continued, she still prepared his meal, served him, and continued her daily chores.

Then one day I overheard my grandfather discussing my grandmother with his friends. He told them, "My wife is magical. She is a blessing to my family. Despite all my anger and shouting, she has never been less of a good woman. That woman has a deep heart, as deep as the ocean, because she has absorbed all my nasty behaviours all these years." At the time, I was flabbergasted. I was lost in a moment.

Then one day I asked my grandmother, "How do you manage to bear, take all our annoying attitudes, and still care, like you don't care about them?"

She smiled and replied, "My child, when a cock crows, you know it's morning. Your question made me happy because it shows you are no longer the little child I used to know. Now listen to me. I am a woman, just as you will someday be. The one who created us [women] made our hearts very deep to accommodate all the bad behaviours from our family members, all the anger, the quarrels. This ability is a special one. I don't know how, but I just feel the bad goes down deep to the extent I feel I lost them, and it gives me the strength to love you all. I may not be able to explain this to you, but know that you are a woman, so don't lose it for no reason."

Then I said, "But Grandpa keeps annoying you all the time, even insulting you."

She quickly cut in and said, "Listen, most times if you are loyal and respectful to your husband, don't take to heart whatever he says to you. Most times they don't mean what they say, and they don't say what they mean. All you have to do is be at your best. Respect him, bearing in mind that respecting your husband may not be easy because most men are annoying. If you already know this, why would you let what they say injure your emotions? And don't listen to what other women may want to tell you. Because they have bigger problems than you, don't trust their judgement. Just do what works best for you."

When I became a woman, I started to understand what my grandmother tried to explain to me. Every woman is born with the ability to absorb things without limit. The only difference is that most women don't know how to let it go down the depths of their beings. Women are naturally at the receiving end with the numerous troubles of taking care of children, doing the house chores, and other things, women are expected to do.

A woman is bound to lose her temper over trivial issues, but I want you to know today that it is your natural duty to absorb all and still be that mother, that woman the environment, family, and society expect you to be—loving, kind, caring, supportive, and above all, a source of joy to your immediate environment. Don't lose it. It's not too much for you. You are as deep as the ocean. Never forget that. Let the annoyances go down, and suppress them with the knowledge you just received. You are the strongest of humankind, the most caring, the most loving, the most kind. Yes, you are emotional, but you *are* the emotions. Your presence should bring sanity. And you don't need to preach equality to be valued. When you show your invisible abilities, every man will place you above himself, not even equal. Most times when my children go to their father for anything, he tells them, "OK, boy. Go talk to your mommy about it." Or, "OK, sweetheart, Mommy will."

Yeah, that is not equality; that is placing right above, "All right, I will talk to my wife about it." This is not equality; this is placing me above. You don't seek equality when you're supposed to be placed above. All you need to do is earn it. Yes dear, earn it. Every man wants to be loved, respected, and honoured as a man. Do these, and see if he doesn't place you above himself and not even try to make you equal.

# 5

# *Find Out Who You Are*

Get to work now. There are over 100 billion things people can do for you, but discovering who you are is not one of them. You have to know who you are, what makes you, you, not who people think they know. In the previous chapter, we learnt some hidden potentials women are born with, so it's time to find out what combination you have inside you. What hidden abilities did nature plant inside you? Awaken them, and put them to use. The result is a better you. Align with what works for you using your own formula. My formula is waking up by 4 a.m., doing the dishes, and preparing breakfast. I prefer my kids have their full dose of sleep.

This may not work for you because we don't have same circumstances around us. Many women lose focus by comparing virtually everything about their families with others. It doesn't work that way. My husband and I may decide to have four kids, and that's fine for us. But it's not going to be fine with for you if your doctor advise to stop at two. I decide to call my husband my Lord and kneel to serve him a cup of water, this may have been influenced by our ancestral origin. It won't make you less respectful if you don't. Hey, this is my life, and you have yours. Stick to what works for you.

Take some time away from your moments of worry, and dig deep into you. Excavate the unrefined natural abilities you have. Refine them. Start learning how to use them. It doesn't matter who gets offended for you being you. Don't expect anyone to help you find you; only you can do this job. It's quite demanding and exhausting, but you need to get working on it as soon as possible because you are not permitted to exist outside the reality of time and space.

*Find Your Purpose*

The word "purpose" means the reason something is done or created, or for which something exists, or a person's sense of resolve or determination. By this definition, you probably want to reiterate the insightful lines in the meaning.

Everything we have been discussing centres around purpose. What is your purpose in life? If you never had the chance to ask yourself this question, now is the right time. Take a few minutes to think about what you think your purpose is, and then come back to this book.

Welcome back. Perhaps you couldn't figure out anything because you don't know for sure what to think. It can seem intimidating at first, but it's simple. Start by asking yourself, "What do I want this year? How do I achieve it? Do I have the means to achieve what I want? Can I withstand the hurdles that come with it? Do I have an alternative? Maybe you should start with all these questions and then pop into reality.

Your purpose should reflect a goal that will leave a mark or a legacy for your children and society. The right time was yesterday, but today is the best time to start digging deep into you.

# 6

## Learn to Let It Go

One of the most important things in life is mastering the art of forgiveness. It is very important, and it is also difficult for many people. The human heart perpetually seeks an unrefined vendetta, a prolonged bitter quarrel with or campaign against someone. The feelings of been cheated and the inability to control the "small steering over the big ship" make it difficult to let go when you are hurt.

When I was a child, I would fight to the end to please the burning desire in me because I wanted to be seen as a heroine. This became a traditional virtue. One day my mother called me and asked me to get her a cup of water to drink, but she insisted I must pass through the wall of the room, not the door or window.

I replied, "Mother?"

"Yes, daughter."

"How am I supposed to do that?"

"You have to try."

I turned and wanted to go through the door. I got a hot spank. Then I knew something had gone wrong. I tried to guess what it was, but I couldn't fathom what it could be.

Then she called my name again. This time she told me, "Go ahead and pass through this wall." I just stood, looking at her. I had no idea what to do. "Sit down now," she told me. "Didn't I ask you to forgive Hannah and let it go?"

"Yes, Ma."

"Why did you go back to fight her?"

"Mom, she started it—"

"Keep quiet," Mom interrupted. "You must learn to forgive, like the dog. I'll tell you a story I was told by the white missionaries who came to our community many years ago. There was a man called Yard. He was a retired veteran of two world wars. He had a dog he named Pulli. Pulli spent over twenty years with Yard. When he became too old and ugly, Yard wanted to dispose of her. He took the dog on a boat trip. When he got to the middle of the river, he threw the dog into the river and hastily paddled away.

"Unfortunately for Yard, Pulli swam beautifully back to the boat. Yard again threw her away, and again, Pulli swam back. This happened several times. The fifth time, Yard became furious and decided to use his paddle to hit Pulli in her head. Yes, he did. Pulli started bleeding. Then came the last strike, that one which broke the camel's back. Yard wanted to hit Pulli again, and as he tried, he fell into the river. Yard never took swimming lessons, so he was drowning. Pulli, a good swimmer, reached out for Yard and pulled him out of the water. She lay on Yard with her tongue out, perhaps waiting for Yard to say he was sorry.

"Now that is forgiveness in the shortest period possible, so daughter, you have got to learn to forgive like the dog."

Women are supposed to be the pools of forgiveness. When someone offends or hurts you, forgiving him or her actually makes you a heroine. It doesn't necessarily mean you are weak. On the contrary, it shows how strong you can be. The school of "Let go" will help you deal with issues that are bound to occur in your home. My mother always told me if you desire to fly, you must give up whatever weighs you down. You need to put down those heavy stones in your mind. Ask the hunter how heavy a bird is, and you will know how to fly.

Letting go also means you must let go of personal guilt caused by a past event or emotional trauma you have held on to for a time. You have to learn the art of forgiving yourself and others, so you can be at peace with yourself and your environment. You don't want to trade this for all the gold in Dubai.

# 7

# *Self-Discipline/Respect*

Self-discipline is unarguably one of the most difficult but easy characteristics of being human. It is the ability to control one's feelings and overcome one's weaknesses. Having control of oneself over certain character traits or behaviours requires some level of self-consciousness and persistent efforts towards adjusting that part of your mind.

Do not allow anyone to deceive you. All things been equal, you get the respect you give to other people in the same value and quantity; it is directly proportional. Do you want people to respect and value you? Then respect and value others. Do to others what you would want them to do to you. There are no mistakes about how reciprocation works.

Remember: the woman in you consistently seeks perfection. Whatever everyone is doing doesn't make it right. What matters involves asking yourself, "What is the right thing to do?" If you know, then do it—even if it means being the only person who does what is right. Just make sure you are not wrong about it.

Another great thing about self-discipline and respect is the fact that society becomes friendly to you. You start to enjoy inner peace and supernatural joy. You need to allow this virtue to flow to your relationships. Who wouldn't want to be happy in his or her relationship?

# 8

# Pick Up the Pieces, and Mend the Broken Parts

Hey, woman, don't wait for me or anyone. Nobody is going to come help you to pick up the broken pieces. *You* need to pick them up! You can never become the woman you should be if you stay too long pondering the broken part of you. You can never bring forth that woman in you if you keep talking about how devastated you are. Yes, you are heartbroken, you are disappointed, you are perplexed, you are shocked and surprised. You never expected such from such person.

Hey, come on. Perhaps you have been dwelling in lies and self-conviction of something you shouldn't have. The only perfection is accepting the fact no one can ever be perfect. You need to stop playing the blame game. Stop blaming people; stop blaming yourself. It's over now. Pick up the pieces and mend them. Then start all over again. Only those who give up are losers. You can start now, like *now!* It doesn't matter what you have lost trying to be better. Just start now.

Some years ago, I had a Japanese friend who lived down the street in my neighbourhood. She worked as a psychiatric nurse. She was in a relationship with this tall, huge, handsome man and always told me how blessed she was to have him. He was supportive and caring and would cook her dinner because she had to take two trains home every day.

They both talked about a Japanese wedding called Shinto, where they would have to exchange nuptial cups, that is called *san san ku do.* "San" means three, and "ku" means nine. So san san ku do means three, three, and nine. The ceremony required them to drink sake three times each from a cup called a sakazuki.

They travelled to Japan to have the wedding. She had to use all her savings as the wedding could cost about $35,000. It was an arduous journey, but they returned after few weeks

One day she got home early to prepare dinner and found her husband on their bed with a young woman they helped to get a job a fortnight ago. My friend was devastated, confused, and didn't know what to think.

When she told me about it, all I could say to her was, "My dear friend, this is a horrible situation for you, I know. But I also know the best thing to do at a time like this is to do nothing." She looked at me as if she wondered if I were insane. I told her to take some time off her work and seek a blue moment, a refreshing outdoor outing. Well, she did and later told me it worked for her. She decided to move on with the marriage. She found happiness in her decision because she picked up her broken parts and mended it.

This may be a difficult activity, but it's sure better for your health. Whatever decision you make today doesn't matter. What matters is that you don't dwell forever in that sober state of unforgiveness. Forgive yourself; forgive whoever needs to be forgiven. Find peace within yourself. The life you have now is a gift. It's precious to you. Value it, cherish it, love it, and don't let anyone steal the joy in it. After all, if you don't forgive them, they feel no pain about the cause. You are the one at the receiving end and feel the weight of anger all day. You become unhappy. This can often lead you to make a decision that may negatively affect you, and you may never be able to correct it. So you must live with it all the days of your life. That is, if it doesn't cost you your life.

# 9

# The Colour of Your Heart

The heart is a very important organ. It is responsible for circulating blood round your body. But that is only the physiological function of the heart. In this chapter, we discuss why you need to be more concerned about your mental health.

Psychologically, the heart does more work than pumping blood all day. This is not a medical journal, so let's look at it from the angle of a woman as a social being. It is often believed that women are the most sensitive gender on Planet Earth.

Being sensitive means much more than the word "sensitive". I do not believe women are the weakest as often claimed by people who do not understand what it takes to be a woman. As a woman, you are strong, brave, courageous. And above all, you are unbreakable. You just didn't know that. You probably didn't know because your society is making you feel otherwise. Your zero-resistance force (RF) for circumstances has flattened your hope. You have read too many wrong books, watched the wrong movies, listened to the wrong tapes, and got the wrong advice.

Now it's time to come home, to return to the true nature of being a woman.

As a woman, most times you do the dishes, the laundry, cooking, and watch over the kids. You do more of the shouting, roll on the floor with them, and clean them up when they get dirty or messy. You console the children when they disagree with each other and attend to them when they need chocolate.

You think about the man, what he will eat when he gets home, advise him when he is confused about what direction to take, and console him when things aren't going the way they should. All of these could be happening at the same time with just one brain, one heart. This may not be same for every woman, and that's OK because there are other activities not mentioned here. The point is that you are not a machine. All these activities can be very demanding. You need a balanced state of emotions to be stable.

Machines are not 100 per cent efficient. They don't work forever. They must undergo maintenance to prolong their lifespan. As for your body, you need to know when it's time to renew yourself—to prolong your lifespan—by working on how to control your state of mind. This will influence the woman you are.

Have you been noticing any mood swings recently? Do you overreact to trivial issues? Do you feel anxious and unsettled? Are you trying to cope with these natural situations? If your answer is yes to any of these questions, you need to learn to control the state of your mind. Tell yourself you are better than this, take a deep breath, and call your name five times in your heart. Ask yourself these questions: "Why am I even worried?" "Is it helping me in any way?" "Am I the only one in the world facing situations? Certainly not. So I think I should calm down and do things that make me happy. If I don't, who will?"

Repeat this simple conversation with yourself over and over again. It helps. The colour of your heart is your state of mind. This is your mental health, and it is important for you to take care of yourself as a woman. Your responsibilities in society require you to be mentally fit all the time.

# 10

# *Awake the Sleeping Giant*

Today's society is a fast-growing one, with technology taking over several functionalities, industries learning new ways to maximize productivity and reduce human labour, and the health sector improving its administration of medical health services. In general, the world is advancing and becoming a small global village, especially with the improvement in information and communication technology. These uncontrollable changes require the active involvement of women in developing maximum productivity.

In the 1950s, men were supposed to work and financially provide for the family, while women managed the home. But after the war, job opportunities opened for women as the world tried to heal. Sexism (prejudice, stereotyping, or discrimination, typically against women, on the basis of sex), especially in relation to social opportunities, was being wiped out, and women became more useful to society.

Today, women are more equal in the work force. While most women believe all jobs are open regardless of gender, some still feel some jobs are not suitable for women. For example, relatively few women actively participate in politics.

The world has evolved and is still evolving. Times have changed, and women's necessity in the growing the work force is increasing. Financial freedom and family support are the major reasons this is happening. It's time to get involved. There is a giant named "I Am Capable" in you. She is sleeping, and you need to wake her up. Wake her up and tell her to get knowledge, get involved, and increase productivity.

*Start Small*

There are thousands of spaces to fit in, but you need knowledge to do so. You want to be a doctor? Get knowledge. You want to be a lawyer? Get the knowledge. You want to be a nurse? Get some knowledge. Whatever you want to be, get the knowledge and contribute to the ever-growing production of the world. There is always a space for you to fit in. Take the first step today. Get registered in any of the learning centres. Make the plan and get the certificate. It's always difficult to start, but trust me, you'll soon get used to it and will have yourself to thank at the end.

Every morning, wake up I Am Capable. She can't be eating your food, staying under your roof for free without getting things done. She can't be quiet when society needs her to talk. She can't be sleeping when her roof is on fire. She has to wake up and work.

The woman in you is far more valuable than you may have known. She is more powerful, she is more resourceful, she is very smart, she is hardworking, she is strong, she is productive, she is resilient, she is focused. She is more than what you used to know. Be that woman in you. There is only one enemy you will have to challenge: your worries and fear of uncertainty.

When my friend Deborah faced the worst moment of her life, I asked her how she was able to cope with the situation. She gave me words that have lived with me and will live with me to the very end of life. She said, "What I have been through in life, I don't wish it for my enemy. All I felt was pain. No one came along when I cried all night. My spirit was broken. Then I told myself, 'Since I can't change the past, time and Energy wasted can never be regained. I will save my energy for what I can change for the future. What matters most is where am going. Where I am coming from can only live in the past. I know I am strong and courageous. I am the best breed ever created for me. As long as the air I breathe remains free, I will keep moving on.'

"I have managed to stay strong through thick and thin, through the hardest moments with hope as my watch word. I had to stop asking those questions that will never have answers."

I encourage you, woman, to be the special breed created for you, to stop asking questions that may never have answers. You can't change the past; you don't have such power. You can only design what the future should look like. As your breath remains free, please keep moving on without self-pity, without depression, without negative energy. Possess the right thoughts, and allow it to drive your way. Bishop Benson Idahosa, of blessed memory, once said, "What you give your attention will most likely give you directions." So I encourage you to stay strong. Don't lose focus. The best anyone can do for you is to talk. The action is all up to you.

# About the Author

Omoyie F. A. K. is a Nigerian-born writer and the author of *The Woman in Me*. She's the wife of a successful businessman and the mother of four children. She's an entrepreneur, a music composer, and an actor. She enjoys writing on the beach and at home in her Scottish garden. Omoyie loves acting in movies, empowering her readers' minds, and teaching women to know they are stronger than they think. Her favourite sentence in *The Woman in Me* is: "There is a giant in you. Wake her up."